You're Not the Only One Who's
Anatomically Correct
'Round These Parts

# You're Not the Only One Who's Anatomically Correct 'Round These Parts

• • •

*Tales of Phallocentrism*

Written and illustrated by
James L. Manchester

Copyright © 2015 James L. Manchester
All rights reserved.

ISBN: 0692524401
ISBN 13: 9780692524404
Bookshelf of the Absurd

This book is dedicated to my first literary mentor, my grandmother. Though I doubt you'd approve of its content, this opus is the result of our many hours spent together, writing stories. Love you forever.

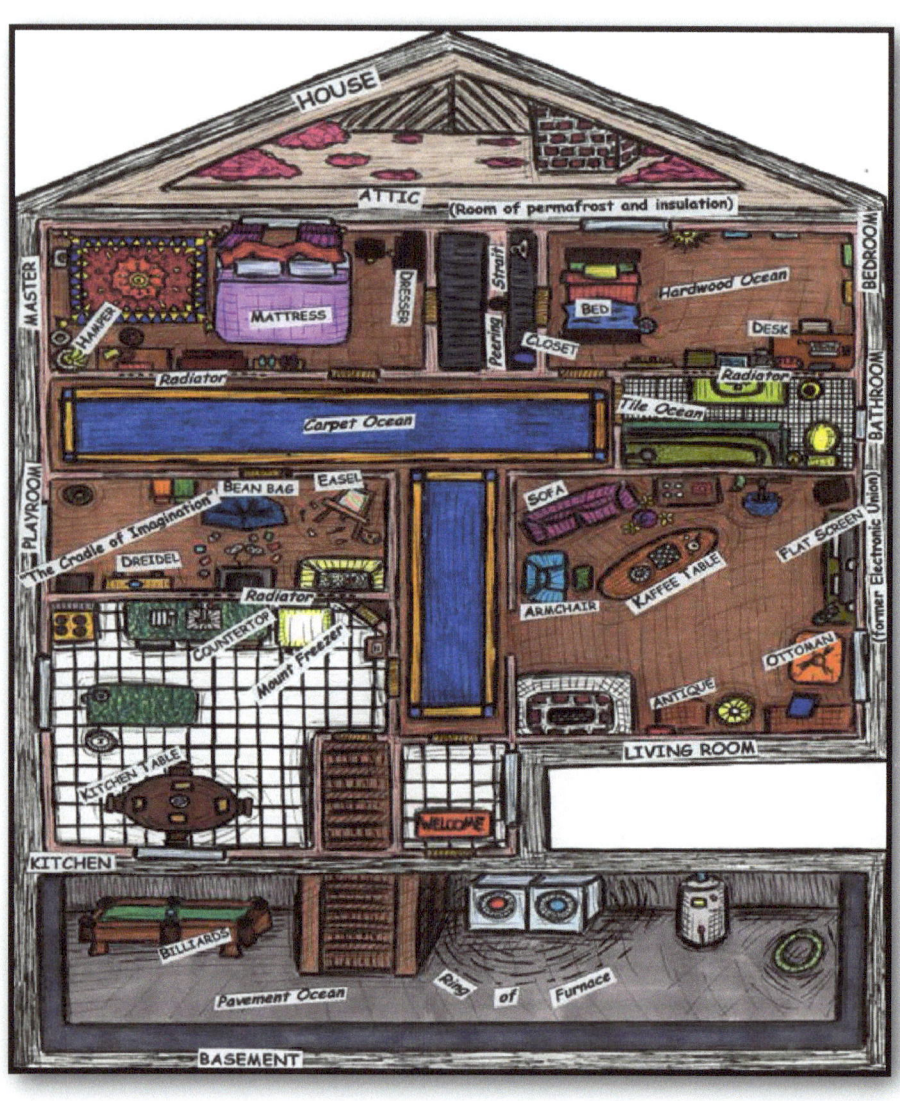

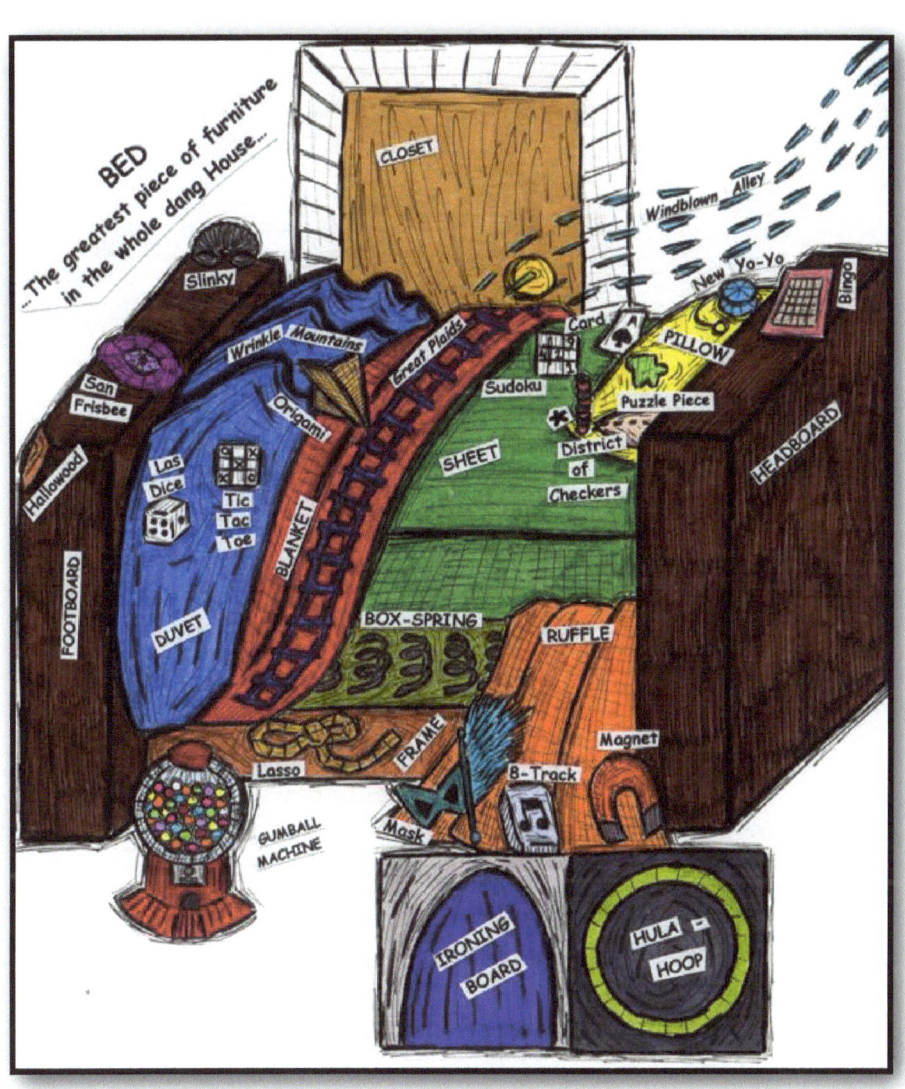

Surrounded by the clutter of an only child, Kid sat on his bed and played with his two best friends, the way he did each day after school let out. Travis T. Bear was the larger of the two, with matted fur and a permanent frown. Some would have called it bitch face, though Travis couldn't help it—it was simply the way he'd been stitched together. Percy Herbert Wimpledon the Third was the stouter of them, with frazzled eyes and a reusable cloth diaper. Poor Wimpy may have been enuretic, but he still cared deeply about his carbon footprint.

On this particular day when our story begins, Kid was acting out a tale in which our furry friends went for a scenic drive, only to wind up stranded somewhere alongside Route Gazillion. What they needed now was a mechanic, and thanks to their lucky stars, Travis just so happened to be one. Popping open the hood, he looked inside and announced in a near squeal, "It's the spark plugs!"

"Your car's not broken," Mom yelled from the other room, enraged and on the phone. Kid paused and listened earnestly. "You're slurring your words and "Pour Some Sugar on Me" is playing in the background. I was born in the eighties too, you know!"

It was the same argument Mom had been having with Dad for the past seven years—the one on missed visits, unpaid child support, and why you shouldn't drunk dial your son at midnight. Mom gasped, shocked by the pejorative gibberish coming from the other line. "Yeah, well you're the male equivalent to that—a real prick!" Mom hung up the phone while stifling a scream. There was simply no state of détente to be found after getting called a "See You Next Tuesday."

Kid remained still, awaiting the knock on his door, which soon followed. Mom peered inside and found her beloved boy looking back at her, holding his furry friends close. Long had Mom thought it not age appropriate for a boy of ten to be fraternizing with two stuffed teddies. Kid's therapist had told her not to be alarmed by such playful solitude, as it was but a form of psychodrama, helping him to work through the unresolved psychosocial crises within the earlier stages of his Eriksonian development. Kid's therapist often said things Mom cared not to hear.

"Dad's not coming today, is he?" Kid asked as he fought back his tears.

"No, darling, he's not," Mom somberly replied.

"Did he fall off the wagon again?"

"*Oh, sweetheart*, your father was never on that wagon to begin with."

Mom felt her heart break little by little on the inside. She worried for the long-term consequences this endless rejection would have on Kid. She feared he might grow up to be an ax murderer or a homosexual.

"Mom, may I put on your stilettos and sing along to your Lady Gaga CD?"

"Of course," Mom replied, grateful that it would most likely be the latter.

Who Kid and Mom were remained of great mystery to the Stuffed Animals, though many believed that they'd been placed there by Bob to watch over them. And if the divine contractor who built The House at a disputed time long ago had left Kid and Mom in charge, who were they to say otherwise? It was for that reason alone the Stuffed Animals didn't declare a state of rebellion and shank them in their sleep—not even when Kid dressed them up in froufrou outfits or Mom left them out in the car on a cold Nor'easter night. Religion had long been a serious matter in The House. Toys killed for Bob.

The chorus to "Marry the Night" echoed throughout the hallways and ushered in our furry friends' return to life. There's only so long a Stuffed Animal can go before shallow breathing causes him, or her, to feel a tad lightheaded. *If you didn't know Stuffed Animals breathe, one might question if you were paying attention in tenth grade biology.*

Travis subtly glanced at Wimpy and spoke his first words of the day. "I swear that kid's gonna grow up a faggot, but that's what happens when you don't got no strong male role model."

To that, the liberal-leaning Wimpy retorted, "Studies have shown homosexuality to be caused by a mixture of genetic predispositions and uterine conditions and, according to certain evolutionary perspectives, serves as a form of population control."

"Shut up with that Ivy League bullshit," Travis snapped back. Our cantankerous chum had an innate mistrust for genetic predispositions, as well as cap-and-trade policies, the use of multisyllabic words, and the deceptive outer layer of a Twinkie. There were no known reasons for this, other than it simply was.

"Oh dear!" Wimpy exclaimed as he stuck a paw beneath the fabric of his diaper. He discreetly conducted the infamous sniff test, only for his hopes of sweat to be dashed by wee. Our little multidisciplinary virtuoso may have held six-and-a-half degrees from the most prestigious universities around, but not even that guaranteed one full bladder control in life.

Travis opened the hood of the '72 Sizzler and looked inside, only to find the timing belt in ruin. Silly Kid had thought the sparkplugs were located under the cylinder head, rather than on top of the crankshaft. Miffed, Travis screamed, "Stick to the hair and makeup and leave the cars to the real men!" Kid may have loved Travis dearly, but the feeling lacked reciprocity. "And next time you try to imitate my voice, don't make me sound like an MTF tranny about to OD on estrogen!"

There was no denying our furry friends were in quite the pickle. Not only was the '72 Sizzler their sole means of transportation, it had also been placed in the care of Travis by a rather pompous malpractice lawyer who barked nouns, rather than full sentences. To our bigoted buddy's good fortune, Tony Akita, Esquire, had a long night of inflating the cost of healthcare, leaving Travis plenty of time to remedy the problem. He quickly pulled out his phone, along with a pack of cigarettes, and called for roadside assistance. Twenty minutes and three cigarettes later, the Anteater brothers pulled up in their pickup, blasting *The Best of Schoolhouse Rock*. Bernie and Scott looked out of the window and exchanged pleasantries with our furry friends.

Travis took the last drag from his cigarette and put it out. "This bad boy needs to be brought in, ASAP. And if you got room, we need to hitch a ride too."

"No problem, just jump on back," Bernie replied. The two Anteater brothers stepped out and chained the Sizzler to the pickup's rear.

"I'll sit up front, if I may," Wimpy articulated. "The back exacerbates my anxiety."

"Suit yourself, pansy," Travis replied as he climbed onto the truck's bed.

In no time good ol' boys Bernie and Scott were going sixty to the sound of "Conjunction Junction." The breeze smacking him in the face, Travis thought out loud, "There ain't nothing better than speeding down the road to a classic." Tied to the antenna, a tattered flag fluttered to-and-fro in the wind. On it was the embossed image of a California King. This was the emblem of Bed, the greatest piece of furniture in the whole dang House—just ask any of the Toys from there, they'd tell you so. Brimming with patriotism, Travis shouted the Bedding motto to a passing pedestrian: "Live free or go fuck yourself!"

The noxious scent of superglue and model paint filled the cardboard auto shop. Empty beer cans piled up high, higher than the racks of tires and break pads, as Travis had long been of the mindset one works better with a buzz. Seated on the stained couch in the corner, Wimpy read the most recent edition of the *New Yo-Yo Times*.

Rolling out from under the car, Travis cracked open a beer. "What's the paper say about the Yodel's trade?"

"I'm not sure, Travis," Wimpy replied, subtly irritated by the interruption. "I'm reading a fascinating article on Dr. Johannes Rockhopper, from the Headboard Institute of Technology, who just cured cancer."

"Boring," Travis roared, wiping the overflow of beer from his mouth. "You know what you should be doing right now, Wimpy—*let me tell you*—you should be watching me, not reading that shit. Maybe you'd learn a thing or two and go get yourself a job rather than just sit around and suck the system's tit dry."

"I have a disability, known clinically as panic disorder, which doesn't allow for me to work," Wimpy calmly retorted. "And to be honest, I find the implication that I'm a moocher highly offensive."

"Don't use that assertiveness psychobabble with me," Travis caterwauled. "I'm not your enabling therapist. I'm your pal. I care about you, and that's why I'm telling you to get off your self-pitying ass and get a job!"

Travis was a proud member of the Go Between'ers, one of Bed's two major political parties and therefore believed disabilities were nothing more than commie propaganda. Wimpy, on the other paw, was a registered Grouper and for that reason thought differently on the matter. Guzzling down the last of his beer, Travis stepped behind the wheel and started the ignition. He rolled down the window and grinned at a downtrodden Wimpy. "Get in and let's go get trashed!"

James L. Manchester

## The Go-Between'ers Party Platform (in their own words)

**\*\*\* Resisting Progress Since 1981\*\*\***

The Sanctimonious Old Bourgeoisie is truly the workers' party, and that's why we support tinkle-on-you economics. When the rich, who are immensely generous, are allowed to keep their money, they use it to create jobs for all them poor folk and teach them an important lesson on the value of "a buck earned." It was, after all, through hard work—not birth, sheer luck, or the willingness to step on others—that they garnered their wealth. For this reason, Go-Between'ers are adamantly opposed to labor unions, who seek to cap the finite amount of money the rich have to help the poor. With all their do good'ing, the rich deserve their five pieces of waterfront property and five respective yachts, to decompress. And like any rational Stuffed Animal will tell you, if not for minimum wage, EVERYONE would have a job.

Moving on, the SOB zealously supports freedom of speech, which doesn't exclude hate speech. If you start putting limitations on hate speech, before you know it, there'll be limitations on other forms of discrimination too. And that brings us to the matter of guns, which, unlike marriage equality, are a right, not just a want—so stop making such a fuss and just be grateful we allow you to live out your profligate lifestyle. Reproductive rights are code for ladies acting like sluts, which will only bring about the degradation of society. Limiting immigration is of fundamental importance as many of these unfortunate immigrants come from war-torn, disease-ridden locations, or even worse, secular, socialist societies. We'd hate to see them alter the very fabric of Bed, and so should you!

Pseudoscientific evidence "refudiates" the theory of HVAC Malfunctioning, just as it did that other unspeakable theory. The House was given to us by Bob, and therefore it's our Bob-given right to use it as we see fit. Go-Between'ers place a high premium on keeping a tight fiscal budget, but the one area we're not willing to cut is defense. Bed needs a strong military to promote our superior values throughout the rest of The House. Trust the SOB; someday they'll thank us for it!

You're Not the Only One...

**The Grouper's Party Platform (in someone's words)**

### Crushing Individualism Since 1917

*Like our name implies, the basis of the Grouper doctrine is groupthink. It's for this reason we support public healthcare and universal higher education. There's no better way to keep the masses dependent on big government than through a single-payer system, and no superior method of indoctrinating the youth into socialism than through a funded four year degree at some leftist, think tank university. Unlike Go-Between'ers, we prefer "lazy and free" over laissez-faire. As your run-of-the-mill vanguard party, we hold control as the premise of our progressive ideology, and that's why we endorse gun control. If everyone had a gun, the whole of society would be safe, but the collective well-being is antithetical to our mission as we're in cahoots with the terrorists.*

*Liberal is a dirty word derived not from liberty but rather from libertine. Just look at our agenda for further proof. Insurance companies should be mandated to provide birth control and abortion to all ladies, as it's the best way to euthanize those minorities the SOB would prefer to simply ignore. Marriage equality isn't about the legal sanction of a loving commitment between two consenting adults, but rather the systematic destruction of the moral cornerstone, which is the institute of traditional marriage. And that's why we fought against the Defense Of Old-fashioned Marriage Act, otherwise known as DOOM. We're unanimously opposed to capital punishment as keeping criminals alive, much like food stamps, simply serves to waste the tax payer's money. Labor laws and affirmative action play an essential role in our platform, as they keep marginalized groups oppressed by the iron law of wages and an unwarranted sense of entitlement, better known as reparations.*

*Groupers hate Bed almost as much as we hate Bob, and that's why we espouse diplomacy over militarism. By doing so, we remove ourselves from the upper echelon of The House stage and help bring about a Remodeled House Order. Our maniacal lust for power is also evident in our acceptance of HVAC Malfunctioning and promotion of wealth redistribution. If you don't see this, it's simply because your czarist professor did well brainwashing you.*

The New Yo-Yo skyline—with its assemblage of devil sticks, juggling clubs, and Art Diablo architecture—stood tall behind our furry friends as they trotted the streets of No Name City. Living in the shadow of greatness had a way of making them feel a tinge secondary at times. Amid the latte drinking and headset adorned Stuffed Animals, Rag Doll sanitation workers went about their job duties. Our bigoted buddy glared contemptuously as they spoke to one another in a language of accented mumbles.

"Friggen Rags everywhere, taking our jobs and expecting us to pay their way."

"Would you prefer to be the one who collects garbage and disposes of biohazard waste?" Wimpy reverberated.

"Fuck that! *What's your point?*"

"They're simply seeking a better life in the furniture of opportunity, where anything is said to be possible through dedication and perseverance, just as our ancestors had been seeking when they migrated here from Living Room."

"But we stole this furniture fair and square. They need to go squat somewhere else."

Many digital clocks and DVR recordings ago, Bed had been a colony of Armchair but gained independence after a lengthy battle. It was, after all, in the words of one famed revolutionary, "absurd for where one lies to be ruled by where one sits." Despite her history, immigration had become a hot-button issue in modern-day, Bedding politics. And like most hot-button issues, our furry friends were in strong disagreement.

Travis and Wimpy stepped inside of the cardboard pub. Beams of light poked through the torn-apart walls covered with periodical clippings and duct tape. Drug dealers, prostitutes, and bums using the last of their collection cups, congregated around the ornamental jukebox and bathroom turned unisex vomitorium. Lenny's had all of the essentials, and nothing more. Travis and Wimpy had been frequenting Lenny's for over a decade—a decade in Stuffed Animal years, that is, which are similar to dog years.

Our furry friends approached their two best drinking buddies, Linus and Leon Lion, at the bar. It was past noon, and therefore little Linus was halfway inebriated. Laid off from his job at the milk crate factories four months earlier, the poor dear had been getting drunk on unemployment ever since. His oafy cousin, Leon, feigned existential indifference while sweeping his frosted bangs from a perfectly manicured bedhead mane. This cool cat spent most of his leisure time Googling the names of obscure philosophers for the sake of name dropping them into future conversations.

"Look, it's Travis and Wimpy," Linus yip-yap-yelped in his thick New Yo-Yo accent. "How the heck is you two?"

Fred Fish, the stoic bartender, rolled his eyes from behind his workstation. "Keep slurring your words, Linus, and I'll have to cut you off."

"Go funk yourself—and that was intentional."

Fred had heard it all before, and mostly from Linus. Mr. Fish had been working at Lenny's ever since his junior year of community college, and after Lenny kicked the bucket, he convinced his accountant brother to cosign the loan, making him the new owner. It had been a busy year for Fred, buying a business and home all in one, and for that reason he chose not to overexert himself with superfluous name changes.

"Another Stale Ale, Leon?" Fred asked.

"Totes, man. Free trade microbrew beer is like socially conscious booze." Such a remark was made each time Leon ordered a drink, as it reminded the others he might be with them, but he wasn't drinking their liquid capitalism.

"Get me the regular," Travis told Fred and lit a cigarette. Our pack-a-day pal cared little for the public ordinance against smoking in highly flammable establishments.

"Nothing for me, thank you kindly," Wimpy concluded. "My doctor recently started me on a new psychotropic for my anxiety and specifically told me to not consume alcohol, or operate heavy machinery."

"Blah, blah, blah," Travis roared. "Who listens to the doctor?"

"Yeah, they're like whores to the pharmaceutical companies, and that's way not cool," Leon interjected.

Wimpy showed them the warning label on the prescription bottle, only for Linus to rip it out from his paw. "If they say not to mix it, it must be a good time!" Linus opened the bottle and ingested a pill soon thereafter.

"There are only enough for the month." Wimpy gasped. "That's one less pill and one more day of acute anxiety ahead of me now!"

"You'll be fine." Travis brushed him off. "It's all in your head." He then followed suit and popped a pill himself. "Hey, Fred, get Wimpy a cold one." Travis handed the bottle to Leon, who shook his head no in return.

"I only use nonsynthetic drugs—like Ketamine."

Our nervous Nelly chum grabbed the bottle from Travis and placed it safely back in his pocket. Wimpy may have had an IQ of 175, but like most Stuffed Animals, he still needed to be heavily medicated just to function. There were many stressors faced by the citizens of Bed which only a mood stabilizer could fix, including, but not limited to, economic recessions, unemployment, war, food allergy distress, the rising debt ceiling, bad-dating posttraumatic stress, terrorism, social media envy, gun-related violence, and status-symbol-induced depression. These were perilous times to be a Stuffed Animal.

"You should totes see my homeopath," Leon suggested.

"Sounds quaky, but the guy ain't so bad." Linus winked. "He even wrote me a script for medical marijuana—for my glaucoma."

"That's not glaucoma." Fred chuckled. "That's just good, ol' fashioned blurred vision." He plopped a beer down in front of a reluctant Wimpy.

"You guys coming over for the game Sunday?" Travis turned to Linus. "I'll get the old ball and chain to take Val with her for the night."

"Val was last week. I'm back with Trish now," Linus confessed. "That gold digger, Val, wanted me to bring her to some fancy-pants restaurant for her birthday. But not Trish, she's never asked me for nothing more than a good romp in the sack. I'd marry the broad if she wasn't such a butterface."

Travis nodded his head in agreement. "They might all look the same in the dark, but not in the wedding album."

"Them queers are mighty gross," clamored the voice on the television in the corner. The four of them turned to see reality TV star and oil spill survivor, Daddy Duck, on the screen.

The screen cut to blond bombshell anchor, Candace Vixen, with her usual reactionary rage. "This duck is a champion for freedom of speech, and he's being badgered by the lefties because of it." Caught off guard, Candace Vixen paused. "Oh, my earring just fell into my cleavage. Don't mind me while I fish it out." Breast deep, she went on with her diatribe. "This is an attack on our civil liberties—there it is! *Nope, that's just the underwire.*"

Wimpy sighed. "This type of overt misogyny is simply abhorrent."

"Totes," Leon agreed. "But you gotta admit—she's got a nice rack."

"Here, here, to the bimbo with the nice rack," Linus cheered.

"I'll toast to that," Travis howled, and lifted his mug. Our status quo ante bellum pal detested the liberal media with all of its sensationalized social issues pushed on the viewer: happy gay couples *at long last* allowed to tie the knot; poor kids with congenital heart disease *finally* having access to much-needed heart transplants; and the welfare queen *eventually* getting herself a job. It was for this reason he watched Foxy News, the only channel free of partisan biases—but that's because conservatism is born in truth, *don't cha know.*

The screen cut to President Orobica as he spoke of affordable healthcare, gun control, and diplomacy. Above the executive goat's head appeared the word *tyrant*, with the channel's slogan, "Even-keeled & Objective" written below him.

"Fucking fascist," Travis growled.

"I tailgated the Purple Fascists once." Leon reminisced. "Or was that the Melancholic Anarchists?"

"Same difference," Travis mumbled back.

"Actually," Wimpy phonated, "Fascism is a right-wing movement, which seeks to gain upward mobility through a strong military, charismatic leader, and doctrine of xenophobia. Fascism and communism are often confused with one another, despite being on opposite ends of the ideological spectrum."

"Shut up!" Travis snapped, causing the automatic response of a stream of pee to dribble down his pal's leg.

The screen cut to business mogul, Darren Hump, whom Travis heralded as the bombastic voice of reason. "This president of theirs isn't from here," The Hump declared and spit loudly to the side. "He might be from Kitchen or the Bathroom, but he ain't from our Bed!"

Now that Candace Vixen had thoroughly berated her own leader, it was time for her to move on to someone else's. Behind her appeared an image of Ping Pong-un, the militant Porcelain Figurine from North Nightstand. "Turning to foreign affairs, flipped-his-lid despot, Ping Pong-un, has threatened to blow Bed up once again. Like we haven't heard this one before—*right, guys*?!" The laughing track followed as Ping Pong-un waved a fist in the air and chanted, "Death to Bed."

"Poor Ping Pong-un," Wimpy remarked.

"You actually feel bad for the flipped-his-lid despot who wants to kill us all?!" Travis scowled. "I never heard nothing more stupider in all my life."

"He's still mourning the passing of his father, Ping Pong-il. This is simply his way of displacing that underlying pain due to a system of poorly constructed coping mechanisms. I do surmise that he'd benefit from intensive grief counseling."

"Maybe we should send him a care package too." Linus jested. "One with them tasty fruits."

"But only if it's from an organic co-op," Leon added. "Not some large, money hungry corporation." And in the spirit of anti-corporatism, he pulled out his Pear™ phone and searched for fair-trade fruit baskets.

"What we should do is level them to the ground," Travis wailed. "And don't give me none of your 'Kumbaya' bullshit."

Poor Wimpy flopped face first against the bar, unconscious and floating in a pool of spilled beer. Travis, Linus, and Leon looked at their fallen comrade and then glanced at one another, unsure of what had transpired.

Fred walked over with a bucket of ice and tossed it inside of the bin. He looked nonchalantly at a comatose Wimpy and said, with a slight lift of the brow, "Maybe you shouldn't mix beer with psychiatric medication after all."

Stuck behind a hippo in a hybrid with a "coexist" bumper sticker, the drive home proved to be a grueling one for Travis. Upon turning onto his plat, he opened up a beer and coasted down the street lined with tin, copper, and stainless steel cookie-cutter homes. Little tykes played behind wax-candle fences, while Rag Doll landscapers trimmed cinnamon bun shrubs. Minivan moms exchanged recipes and gossip in front of their cupcake-topper mailboxes as middle-management dads returned from long days of displaced aggression.

Travis and his common-law wife, Moona Lisa Cow, had moved to the suburbs two years earlier after finding a great deal on an in-law apartment. Moona Lisa had given Travis the ultimatum: "Buy me a home, *or else.*" And in the spirit of compromise, he rented her one instead—though it wasn't just any home he got her but rather a newly renovated colonial revival. The elderly Cockatoos had blown through their entire savings in order to have the most beautiful home in the neighborhood—that is, until the Frogs renovated their Mock Tudor. And all it cost them was their retirement *and* child's college fund. This was suburbia. This was to what all Stuffed Animals aspired.

Our blue-collar buddy waved to Gail Golden-Retriever and Janis Skunk, who politely snubbed him and continued on with their brisk jog. Travis had never been all too fond of Gail Golden-Retriever and thought her, like most with hyphenated last names, a tad self-important. Head of the home-owners' committee, Gail wasn't above abusing her power. Following a tiff with Charlotte Bunny, she vindictively banned rainbow sprinkles. Now worried that chocolate sprinkles might be next, Melissa Moose had been schmoozing her ever since. If Travis had been a home-owner himself, he, too, would have feared her. But Travis was a nothing more than lowly renter, and therefore felt at liberty to slam down on the horn and yell out the window: "You smell like wet dog!"

Travis pulled into his driveway only to see his neighbors, the Naked Dolls, doing the very same. Our fluffy antihero loathed the Naked Dolls, as did everyone else on their street. The Naked Dolls didn't seem to have the same problems as most Stuffed Animals: there wasn't any bad credit, infidelity, or schizophrenic relative to be found. Not to mention they were always nude. Hopeful to avoid small talk, Travis grabbed his six-pack—minus one—and darted across the freshly manicured dough lawn.

"Howdy, neighbor! How are you this swell day?"

Travis begrudgingly mumbled an unintelligible response and turned to see Dick Naked Doll standing with his wife, Joyce, and their 2.5 kids. Dick was a company man who sold cancer-causing face creams for Formalde Young. Joyce was a homemaker and the founder, president, and sole member of the town's temperance movement. Susie was a straight-A student, track star, and peer mentor. Billy was a baseball fan and proud Webelos scout. Jacob was an aborted fetus they'd adopted and carried around in an urn.

"I hope you and Moona Lisa will be joining us this Tuesday for the church raffle!" Joyce exclaimed.

"It's going to be super-duper fun, Mr. Bear!" Susie squeaked. "Ice cream sundaes and all!"

"But none of that vile gambling or those glutinous libations," Dick added.

"So it's BYOB?" Travis asked.

"You're a real hoot and a half!" Joyce chuckled. Dick and Susie followed her lead as Billy simply stood there with a sourpuss look on his face.

"Don't mind Billy," Dick interjected. "He's down in the dumps over losing the game. But after dinner we're going to play a game of scrabble. That should lift his spirits."

"Jeez, Dad, you always know how to make things better," an elated Billy exclaimed.

"It's a skill that comes with age. You'll see someday, son."

Travis watched as the 4.5 of them succumbed to a group hug. He quickly excused himself.

"Have a nifty night," Dick called out. "Hope to see you next Tuesday."

"The same to you," Travis grumbled back, "Fuckwad!"

Upstairs in their apartment above the plastic garage, Moona Lisa Cow sat with her sister, Mona, watching reality TV and spending money she didn't have. Moona Lisa worked part time as an aerobic instructor at the gym down the street, teaching spin, while Mona worked full time as a starving artist, making life-size replicas of deceased poets out of elastic bands. And like so many Stuffed Animals, their days revolved around the scripted lives of others: morning coffee with addicts in rehab, eleven o'clock workout with hoarders, dinner with pageant moms and their future anorexic daughters.

It was three in the afternoon, and socialite Sally Sock Monkey was on the screen. Feigning surprise at her boyfriend's proposal, Sally hugged her sisters, Sasha and Stacy, while their mother, Sandra, welcomed Greg to the season.

"I want her thighs," Moona Lisa said, pushing her plate of kale away.

"I want her bank account," Mona rebutted, chowing down on two heaping servings.

Moona Lisa looked with contemplation at the half-off cubic zirconia vase on her computer screen. She didn't need it, just like most of the eclectic crap filling their place. But it helped fill a void, so she pressed purchase. "This show makes me depressed." Moona Lisa sighed. "My life sucks compared to hers."

"Speaking of sucks, did you see that video of her online and the way she deep throated that guy's tail?"

"No. Seeing her naked would only make me hate my body more."

Mona rolled her eyes and dug into her sister's portion. Mona had been attending a support group to help her come to terms with her robust build: "Big is beautiful" had become her mantra of choice. Moona Lisa, on the other hoof, was determined to undermine her genetic proclivity and remain forever slim. She wanted nothing more than to be the Twiggy of Bovine.

"This salad could use something more than a lemon wedge," Mona complained. "I thought the whole kale trend was going out?"

"Some things will always be classic, like the little black dress and cocaine. Kale just so happens to be one of them."

The front door opened and none other than Mr. Cantankerous stepped inside, mumbling about the nudist Goody-Two-Shoes next door. Ignoring both his common-law wife and sister-in-common-law, Travis was quickly drawn to the TV. "Damn, Sally Sock Monkey is hot!"

"Thanks for commenting on how she looks without saying a word about me!" Moona Lisa shouted. "Do you have any idea how hard I work to look this good? Do you even know how hungry I am? I have four stomachs, don't forget!"

"Now that you mention it—I'm starving! You make me dinner yet?"

Moona Lisa stormed off and slammed a few doors along the way. Taking that to mean no, Travis raided the ice-box and found a freezer-burned pizza in the back.

Mona shook her head in disbelief. "You're so insensitive."

"Don't start with me," Travis snapped back and put the pizza in the microwave, for five minutes longer than advised. "You're always coming here, eating my food, and filling my girl's head with your feminist bullshit—just because you don't got a guy."

The fact that Mona was a lesbian was irrelevant to Travis, as he believed every lady wanted a guy, even the ones who didn't. "My entire family hates you." Mona sneered. "My mother cries herself to sleep thinking of the damage you're doing to Moona Lisa's self-esteem."

"Your mother's a whore."

"My father's planning to take a hit out on you. He thinks it's worth doing time."

"I could kick your father's ass any day."

"We hired a professional and had an intervention with her, but not even that worked! She doesn't think she deserves better than you. You did a real number on her, Travis!"

"Go graze a field, fatso!"

The microwave beeped. Mona pulled the soggy pizza out and screamed after burning herself. Travis keeled over, laughing. Resourceful, Mona pulled the cord, lifted the microwave up, and brought it with her as she stepped out the door. The last laugh had been had, and it had been had by her.

In what had become a nightly ritual, Moona Lisa stood before her *Valley of the Dolls* medicine cabinet and sorted through the countless prescriptions and over-the-counter drugs. There were bottles of Wellbutrin, tabs of Adderall, doses of Trazadone, pills of Xanax, milligrams of Vicodin—something to mask each ailment and offset every side effect. Popping a sleep aid, Moona Lisa washed it down with a vodka chaser. She then took an extra Xanax and rationalized that it had a short half-life.

Moona Lisa gazed at her vacant reflection, lost in the mirror, baffled by what she saw staring back. Brittle black spots, hollowed horns, sagging udder—she wasn't the cow she'd once been. This wasn't the life she'd dreamed of for herself. She'd dreamed of the ballet, longed for Tchaikovsky, but gave all of that up for the false security of a conventional life. And now she no longer had the ability to dream—in part due to the way psychotropics interfere with REM cycle.

Entering their room, Moona Lisa found Travis measuring his groin fur with a ruler. He gleefully announced to her that he had grown a whole half centimeter.

"Get out!" she barked. "I'm still mad at you."

"Then let's have make-up sex. That always makes things better."

"You're clueless."

"Would it help if I said sorry?"

He soon found that it did not. Twenty minutes later, Travis had been cast to the couch with a cold beer in paw and soft-core porn on the tube. He hooted and hollered as two heavily augmented blow-up dolls tossed water on one another and giggled over the way it tickled their inflatable areolas. But as titillation wore off, Travis realized this was nothing more than a poor substitute for intimacy. "This ain't the stuff wet dreams are made of!" Travis exclaimed. "It's the stuff blue balls are made of."

In search of an escape, Travis went to his favorite watering hole. There, he told Fred his many woes over a pint of swill. "I give her my money, let her buy all the crap she wants, tell her she looks hot when she wants me to lie, tell her she don't when she wants me to be honest. What more could the broad want?"

Fred placed a halfway polished glass down and looked up longingly. "Perhaps she wants a strong shoulder to lean on in times of tumult, a warm smile to wake up to in the morning, a quiet ear to listen to her at the end of a trying day, a supportive paw to hold from now until eternity. Ladies want all sorts of things, or so I'm told."

"I don't know, Fred. Maybe I'm missing something."

"That's also possible. How about another round to drown your confusion?"

"You're a good friend, Fred."

"It's a dirty job, but somebody's gotta do it."

"I'll screw you for fifty Play-dough," said the androgynous voice from the recesses of the cardboard pub.

Travis turned to see Tammy the Town Hooker standing there in a halter top and mismatched fishnets. Yellow and black strands fell from her pom-pom weave down into her face. Both mesmerized and repulsed, he watched her simulate fellatio on the token cigarette hanging from her mouth. Fancying himself a libertarian of sorts, Travis fully supported the rights of prostitutes and their johns. But Tammy the Town Hooker carried a high price tag: three months to be exact. Dressed incognito for a luau, Officer Pork hid in the corner. The getup wasn't fooling Travis though; he could spot a pig from just one look at its snout.

"Sorry, but that's a criminal offence."

Tammy the Town Hooker turned to Officer Pork. "How many times do I gotta tell you, Hal, I'm not gonna marry you?"

"That's fine, toots." Officer Pork smiled and pulled out his cuffs. "I'll just keep on arresting every scumbag trying to deflower you, my misguided petunia, until you say I do."

Like a perverted Aesop's Fable, wherever Tammy the Town Hooker went, Officer Pork did follow.

It was then that Fred had the most ingenious of ideas, as he often did at such times. "Travis, how about you pay Tammy's tab? And Tammy, how about you have sex with Travis out of appreciation for his generosity?"

Both parties agreed to the terms. Travis pulled out his wallet and placed the appropriate amount of Play-dough down, while Tammy the Town Hooker whispered sweet nothings in his ear. "I'll let you do me raw if you get me a shot of So Co and lime."

"Don't do this to me, Tammy," Officer Pork pleaded. It didn't matter how much love he had for Tammy the Town Hooker though, not when she lacked that very same love for herself.

"No golden showers, and *Tallahassee* is my safe word," Tammy the Town Hooker said and threw back a shot of So Co and lime. "We all got our limits."

Out in his pickup and sprawled across the front seat, our lusty pal was in the throes of bad sex. From his present position, Travis found it difficult to discern whether Tammy the Town Hooker was pregnant or if she simply had a distended liver. He knew not whether she was a weasel, bagger, or aged-beyond-her-years lynx. The one thing he was assured was that when it came to her trade, Tammy the Town Hooker lacked a work ethic.

Thrusting against her limp body, Travis grunted, "Take it all."

Stifling a yawn, she asked, "You think we can get another drink after this? I'm losing my buzz."

"*Umm, sure*, give me five."

Travis fought to keep his stamina despite the added pressure, but then she pulled out her phone to set the alarm, and he was done for. Tammy the Town Hooker had been around the block, and knew full well that guys lie. "Chop, chop," she ordered. "You're on the clock."

One week later, Travis found his nether region a tinge irritated. But what started as a nine-o'clock itch, soon become a midday inflammation. Rightfully concerned, he asked Wimpy, who had half a medical degree, for professional advice. His neurotic pal, who'd dropped out of medical school halfway through and therefore was allowed to diagnose, but not treat, told Travis to seek immediate help. Due to a pre-existing condition, our uninsured and bow-legged chum had no other option but to visit the community clinic located in the dodgy part of town. There he sat amid bilingual posters for food assistance programs, and attempted to self-diagnose via the web. Bombarded with gonorrhea, trichomoniasis, and herpes simplex two, Travis found solace in knowing one thing alone: "At lease it ain't HIV. Only homos and junkies get that."

"That's a fallacy," Wimpy retorted. "HIV is a simian virus affecting anyone, and not isolated to male homosexuals, intravenous drug users, and hemophiliacs."

"Them hemophiliacs are just as bad as the queers and junkies if you ask me!" Travis huffed loudly. As a mere cub, our encephalitic pal had attended an abstinence-only school and therefore knew none the wiser.

Travis was taken to the exam room where the burley Dr. Raccoon assessed his groin. And to his great relief, cotton-eyed Joe was nowhere to be found. "You have dust mites," the doctor informed Travis. "I'm going to prescribe you a topical cream and recommend ten minutes in the dryer set at 105 degrees Celsius, permanent press preferably."

Confused as to why dust mites hadn't been included in Wikipedia's list of venereal diseases, Travis chose to see the silver lining. "I told my pal it wasn't HIV. Only homos and junkies get that. Right, Doc?!"

Dr. Raccoon folded his arms and sternly replied, "I take offense to that, Mr. Bear."

"Sorry, Doc, I didn't know. I got a cousin who got hooked on oxy after a car accident. It can happen to anyone."

"That's not the part I found offensive!"

It was then that our feebleminded friend realized to which segment of the homos-and-junkies demographic Dr. Raccoon belonged. Slightly embarrassed, Travis asked in a low tone: "You didn't, *uhh*, get turned on during that exam, did you, Doc?"

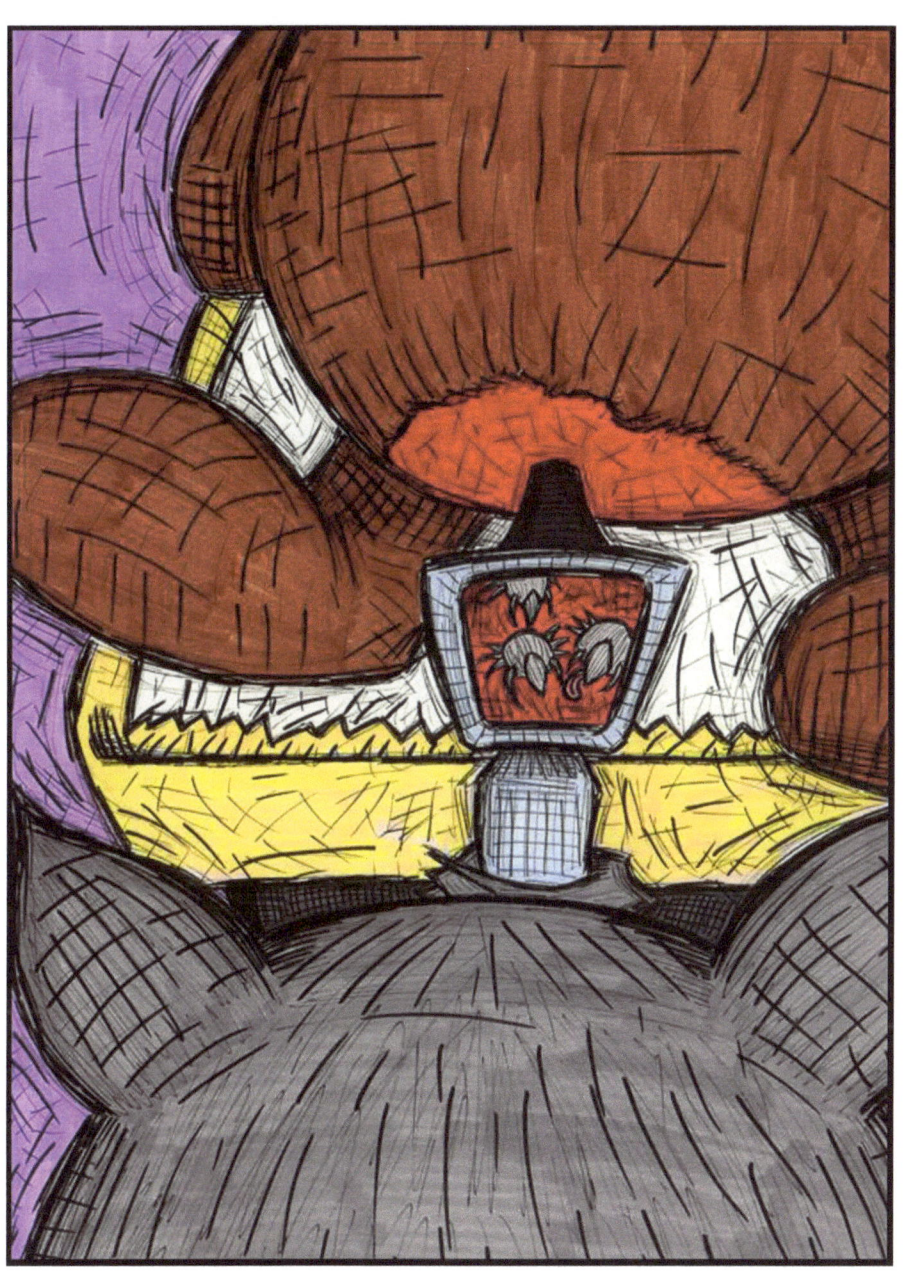

Travis returned home soon after, reluctantly ready to come clean to Moona Lisa. His initial thought was to keep silent, though knowing she may have already been exposed, feared her reaction come the tertiary stages of dust mite infection. Throughout the span of their courtship, Moona Lisa had sought retribution for her lover's many transgressions in the most dubious of ways. There was their fifth anniversary when he invited the guys over for the game, and she burned his work uniform the following morning; the time he bought her regular cola—not diet—and she changed the clocks, causing him to miss his flight to Las Dice for Al's bachelor party; or that one occasion when he recorded late night over her recital video, culminating in enough flax-seed being put in his food to land him on the can for a week straight. Moona Lisa's wrath was like a French epistolary novel: revenge was a dish best served cold and even better when topped with a laxative.

Travis turned the TV off during the middle of her workout routine and spoke with trepidation. "Moona Lisa, baby, I gotta tell you something…I boned some whore last week and caught dust mites."

"Sucks to be you."

"Let's cut the passive-aggressive bullshit and get it over with, okay?!"

"It's not a big deal, Travis," Moona Lisa said with apathy and continued on with her crunches. "It's not like you *actually* cheated on me."

"Yeah, I did. I did to her what I do to you once a year on my birthday."

"You gave her rug burn?"

"Yeah, we had sex."

"No, you didn't!" Moona Lisa screamed. "You can't have sex because you don't have a penis!" To that she jumped up and stormed off in her usual fashion, slamming random doors along the way. It now appeared that idiocy—not infidelity—was really what got Ms. Cow mad.

"She's right," Travis whimpered, as an epiphany befell him. "I don't have a penis."

Within his hour of need, our grief-stricken chum turned to his pals at the cardboard pub. "All these years, I've been telling myself if I twirled it a little to the left, it'd be a penis, when in fact, it was nothing more than matted fur. It's like I've been living a lie."

"Damn, Travis, I thought you knew," Linus sympathetically slurred. "Whenever you'd say, sit on my cock, suck my man-meat, stroke my shlong—I thought you were being, *ahhh*."

"Figurative," Wimpy interjected. "There's a myriad of benefits to not having a penis, Travis, such as a lack of testosterone poisoning and inappropriate erections." The asexual Wimpy had long found the way males glorified their genitalia—be it imagined or not—enigmatic.

Lost in thought, Leon spoke of what life would be like if only he'd been given a Johnson. "If I had a penis, I'd play with it all day long."

Linus slapped his cousin on the back. "I bet you would, you dirty bird!"

Unbeknownst to them, two bird patrons—one spry pigeon and one elegant dove—were seated at the table behind. Enraged, the pigeon yelled out to Linus: "Bigot!"

"Everyone's so fucking sensitive these days!" Linus jumped off his stool and made a few aggressive gesticulations. "You wanna take this outside, asshole?!"

The dove rested a gentle wing on her lover and reminded him to be the bigger bird. Leon leaned closer to our furry friends and whispered, "He often overcompensates—totes because he doesn't have a penis."

Travis turned to the drink-making senex. "How you deal with it, Fred?"

"Well, as you probably know, fish have internal testes. So I tell myself it's up there, along with my intangible balls, and blame it on erectile dysfunction. It helps to ease the pain."

The television in the corner caught their attention. On it the queen of daytime TV, Winny Elephant, told her audience to tune in next time for when she'd reveal both the meaning of life and how to host a fabulous dinner party. Leon, Linus, and Wimpy glanced at one another with that eureka look.

"You should totes go on *The Winny Elephant Show*."

"Yeah, that bitch knows everything!"

"The book she recommended, *It's Not So Bad Outside Today*, helped me overcome agoraphobia."

Our furry friends caught the next train to the city of Sudoku, and once there, made their way to the cattle call. While Travis filled out a questionnaire on his antidepressant regimen and sexual abuse history, Wimpy scanned the room for the one Stuffed Animal with any pull, the casting director. Pushing through the masses of transgendered antelope bucking it out, trashy rabbits seeking paternity tests, and opportunistic donkeys wanting book deals, they made their way toward the lanky giraffe in a blue miniskirt. Awe struck, Wimpy recognized the bird she was talking with as none other than Dr. Johannes Rockhopper, the esteemed Rocky Road Scholar and Noodle Prize Winner who cured cancer.

Travis, however, was a tad more difficult to impress. "My penis trumps his cancer any day of the week." Quickly stepping between them, he shouted, "Hey, lady, I just found out I don't got a dick, and I'm having a hard time dealing."

"No pun intended," Wimpy interposed.

Out of second nature, the casting director told him to fuck off before giving thought to what a teddy bear looking for a penis might do for ratings. "The viewers are going to eat this up, no pun intended!" the casting director exclaimed. She told Travis to be ready in five and then informed Dr. Rockhopper of the change in plans. "You've been bumped. Sorry."

"This is an outrage," Dr. Rockhopper protested. "You're picking this salacious debris over a medical breakthrough! I demand to speak with Winny Elephant on this matter right now!"

To that the casting director pulled out her walkie-talkie and called for security. Moments later, two muscular walruses, with Fu Manchu mustaches and veneer tusks, marched over. Wimpy watched in dismay as they manhandled the belligerent intellectual, forcefully dragging Dr. Rockhopper away.

"If anyone can help you find a penis, it's Winny," the casting director assured Travis. Enraptured, he turned to Wimpy and exclaimed, "I'm gonna get my manhood back!"

From hate mongers to sex offenders, the queen of daytime TV had encountered some rough individuals during her twenty-five-year run, though none quite like Travis T. Bear. Seated across from a taken aback Winny Elephant, our crass friend told her, and her viewership, the details of his ordeal. "After leaving the homo doctor at the welfare clinic that day, I said to myself, 'Travis, you gotta do the right thing and come clean to the old ball and chain about that skank you screwed.'"

"*Your wife, you mean?*" Winny questioned.

"If you wanna get technical, but there ain't no ring on it."

"Still, she must have been heartbroken by your disclosure."

"You'd think, but not really. She's the one who told me I don't got the parts for it to count." Travis winked at the camera. "Who knows, guys, maybe your dead weight will do the same for you."

In the spirit of both damage control and product placement, Winny spoke over him, "*The Winny Elephant Show* does not endorse infidelity, and when engaging in sexual outercourse, you should always use protection, such as Saran, Bed's most trusted wrap." Winny turned to the audience and posed the question, "Who else here feels the same as Travis? Who else here dreams of having a penis?"

To the dismay of the many wives, girlfriends, sisters, mothers, and daughters who'd dragged their special guys along with them, the males in the audience slowly began to raise their various appendages. Tears were shed and hugs freely given as their secret heartache was at long last made known.

Winny turned to Travis and softly spoke, "It appears, Travis, that you're not alone."

James L. Manchester

Life changed dramatically for our neutered pal following his public confession. Charitable events were held in his honor, celebrities took him as their trending cause, and the media scrutinized his every move. Darren Hump expressed solidarity by stating that despite acting like one, he, too, lacked a penis. Sally Sock Monkey was spotted wearing a T-shirt with the words *Support Travesty*. Even washed-up child star, Pinocchio, came forward on his own euphemistic journey to becoming a real boy and how he wound up with an expandable nose due to the conservative times. From the looks of it, that Geppetto was a real size queen too!

Politicians soon jumped on the bandwagon. In the rare occasion of bipartisan agreement, both Groupers and Go-Between'ers supported his right to have a penis—the latter stating it should be used *only* in the context of traditional marriage. And with publicity came controversy as the moral right and feminists spoke out against Travis, whom they deemed the embodiment of both moral impropriety and phallocentrism.

But Travis was more than just a fad. He was the very face of a movement. From Headboard to Footboard, candle-light vigils were held in his honor as a silence had been broken. Stuffed Animals came out of the genitalia closet in what academics coined the Travis T. Effect. The medical community stated that such an inclination was but a variation, rather than deviation, on the sexual spectrum—similar to being a Kinsey Three. Comparative studies showed that Stuffed Animals were the only Toys in The House who lacked genitalia, though that hadn't always been so. There had once been a time when they, too, had the same parts as Rag Dolls and Rubber Duckies. Sadly their privates had been removed in the early days of Bed, when certain puritanical forces outlawed drinking, dancing, and anything else remotely close to fun. Many Stuffed Animals eventually lost sight of this fact and entered into a state of collective denial. This had more than likely occurred during the Rufus Raven Administration, when everything else—from poverty to the postmodern plague—was being ignored.

Never had Travis imagined that he'd cause such a ruckus, when all he'd ever really wanted was a shlong.

Life may have improved for Travis T. Bear, but it only worsened for poor Moona Lisa Cow. All she heard from her common-law hubby these days was penis this, cock that. Each and every attempt she made to voice her dysphoria fell upon deaf ears as he simply said she suffered from penis envy. How Moona Lisa longed for the days of old with its unremitting bigotry and right-wing rhetoric!

Plopped down on the couch, she sought solace in *The Hush-Hush*, a popular self-help book on how negative thinking gets you what you want due to the Law of Irony. Practicing her frowning techniques, Moona Lisa glanced at Travis counting the number of likes on his Fuzzbook page and felt a grimace come to her naturally.

The doorbell rang. Upon answering it, Travis found a stocky wolf, dressed in khaki shorts, with two letters in his paw. "Delivery for Travis T. Bear."

"That'd be me."

"Just sign here and here," the delivery guy said, asking for his autograph. "I saw you on *The Winny Elephant Show* and wanna say thanks for giving us a voice."

"We gotta stick together, brother."

Moona Lisa sighed loudly as the two of them fist pumped. Travis and the delivery guy chuckled in return, together blaming it on penis envy.

The first letter was from his publisher and included both a large advance and a ghost-writer named Bill to help with the creative process. The second letter was from Winny Elephant, Inc., regarding what was possibly the best news he'd ever received.

"Shit, you're not gonna believe this," Travis screeched. "They found me a penis!"

Moona Lisa tossed her hoofs up in the air and lamented, "Just when life couldn't get any worse, it did."

Travis woke from his anesthesia nap several hours post-operation. The doctor and nurse stood near, closely monitoring he who was the first successful penile transplant ever. Our doped-up pal instantly recognized Dr. Raccoon, whose surname was less than common, as the same Dr. Raccoon who'd diagnosed him with dust mites. Urology, family medicine, podiatry—being the only physician in town was the making of a monopoly.

Taken by a fit of laughter, Travis exclaimed, "Figures they'd hire a homo for a job like this!"

Ashley Flamingo, RN, looked at Dr. Raccoon with mounting concern. "He's speaking nonsensically. Do you think he suffered a stroke during the procedure?"

Dr. Raccoon shook his head while Ashley assessed Travis for facial drooping. "No, sadly that's just *him*—Mr. Bear, there are some important Toys who want to speak with you following the unveiling. And once you're finished with the press, your friends are here as well."

Members of the media poured into the hospital room when suddenly a pair of gangly arms pushed through the mass of flashing cameras and two-bit hack journalists. Dressed to the nines and ready for a photo op, Moona Lisa stepped forward with Wimpy by her side. "Out of my way, paparazzi! If anyone's gonna see my man's member first, it's gonna be me!"

Dr. Raccoon pulled the sheet off and exposed a fully erect, twelve-inch penis, protruding out from a pair of johnnies and held in place with plaster of Paris. Everyone in the room *oohed* and *aahed* at the dark chocolate shower-rather-than-grower before them.

Dr. Raccoon cleared his throat and explained the medical reasons for both its size and pigmentation. "Prosthetic penises come in two different models, flesh tone and ebony. We took the initiative and chose the larger one."

"It's monolithic!" Wimpy marveled.

"So that's what they look like in real life." Moona Lisa gasped.

Travis winked at his common-law wife. "It's all for you, babe, but mostly for me."

Once fully recovered, Travis was ready to put his newfound penis to good use. And that's exactly what he did, lost in his lover's embrace. His lover, however, was not Moona Lisa Cow, but rather an inflatable call girl he'd ordered online. Buried deep within her vinyl orifice, our well-endowed pal rolled his tongue around, when a whistling sound suddenly interrupted them. They turned to see Moona Lisa at the threshold, dressed in a sultry corset and flashing her udder.

"Who's that?" the call girl questioned.

"That's my main chick. Don't worry—she ain't the jealous type. We're polyamorous."

Moona Lisa spoke with seduction on her tongue. "I found a few loose threads down there while shaving, and after pulling them, it looks like you're not the only one who's anatomically correct 'round these parts."

"Hot dang," Travis shrieked. "Let's do it!"

The two of them turned to look at the inflatable escort.

"Beat it, bitch!" Moona Lisa scowled.

"Yeah, don't be a fake cock block," Travis added.

Dejected, she quickly got dressed and parted with the words, "Just because I was manufactured as a masturbatory aid, in no way means I lack feelings."

Once alone, Moona Lisa flung herself on top of her lover. Travis inserted his big black dong into her newly formed vaginal cavity. Wanting to surprise her, he pressed the on switch. It turned out that not only had he been given a prosthetic penis, but a vibrating one to boot. Right as he was about to erupt with ejaculatory fluids and battery acid, Moona Lisa screamed out in agony. Stuffing flew into the air, along with her torso, as his shlong tore through the circumference of her midsection. Her mutilated loins still fixed to him, Travis looked to find Moona Lisa's more cerebral half on the floor, in a state of delirium. He quickly dialed the emergency hotline with but one thought on his mind: "Shit, my work uniform is really gonna get burned now!"

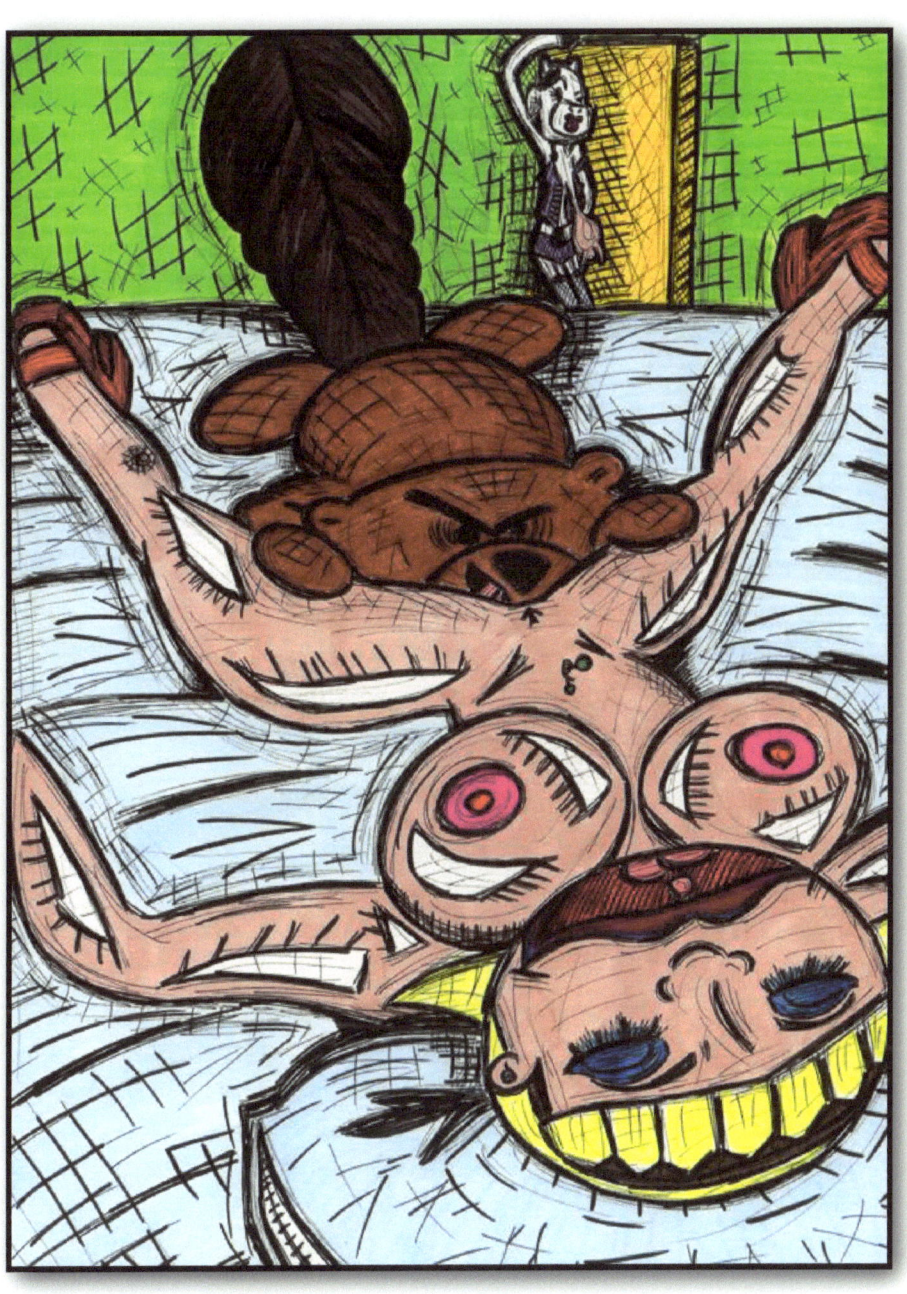

Travis returned soon thereafter to *The Winny Elephant Show* and told the queen of talk TV all about what life was like with a penis. "There were some complications, and I had to cut it off," he confessed. "Yup, that's right. I've gone and been castrated."

Sounds of horror echoed throughout the audience as Stuffed Animals fainted in droves. Winny's eyes barely popped right out of their sewn sockets. Moments later, security wheeled Moona Lisa out across the stage. Stitched back together and snowed from opiates, she babbled nonsensically.

"And here she is, my gal, Moona Lisa," Travis gleefully announced. "She's the one I cut it off for, 'cuz that's what guys do for the ladies they love."

Pleased with his pro emasculation message, the females in the audience cheered him on with a standing ovation.

Travis continued, "It's funny, Winny—for as long as I can remember, the only thing I wanted in life was a dick. But once I got one, I realized that's not what I really wanted. What I *really* wanted was what I had all along, this broad right here." The lights dimmed. Travis kneeled down before his incapacitated lover and pulled out a ring. "Moona baby, let's make this last a lifetime, or till we get divorced, whatever comes first."

To that Moona Lisa let out an unintelligible sound, along with a stupefied smile. Drool dribbled down the side of her face as she nodded off. The collective sound of *aww* was heard. It very well may have been the date rape of marriage proposals, but it was nonetheless taken to mean "yes."

Travis stood up and looked at the camera for his closing moment. "Of all the important things I've learned, the most importantest is this: a guy ain't measured by the size of his penis but rather by his unwillingness to let his penis get in the way of doing the right thing."

Winny smiled and said with the utmost affection, "I should have gone with the guy who cured cancer."

And that right there is the moral of this rather pointless story.

James L. Manchester

James L. Manchester resides in frigid New England, though he dreams of giving it all up for drizzly London. Mr. Manchester's academic background is in psychology and philosophy, and he therefore lacks a real job. James is far too young to be this cynical, yet far too old to still be playing with stuffed animals.

www.ingramcontent.com/pod-product-compliance
Lightning Source LLC
Chambersburg PA
CBHW041642090426
42736CB00034BA/12